KETO-RESET

DIET

COOKBOOK

(A BEGINNER'S GUIDE):

Top New 21 DAYS Ketogenic Recipes to Help Achieve Your Optimum Metabolism and Shred Fat Forever.

By

Dave Miller

Copyright © 2019, By: **Dave Miller**

ISBN-13: 978-1-950772-15-5
ISBN-10: 1-950772-15-2

All Rights Reserved. No part of this publication may be reproduced in any form or by any means, including scanning, photocopying, or otherwise without prior written permission of the copyright holder.

Disclaimer:

The information provided in this book is designed to provide helpful information on the subjects discussed. The publisher and author are not responsible for any specific health or allergy needs that may require medical supervision and are not liable for any damages or negative consequences from any treatment, action, application or preparation, to any person reading or following the information in this book.

THE KETO-RESET DIET COOKBOOK

Table of Contents

INTRODUCTION .... Error! Bookmark not defined.
   Lose Weight by Achieving Optimal Ketosis .... Error! Bookmark not defined.
      TIPS TO GET YOU STARTED ON THE KETO DIET .... Error! Bookmark not defined.
THE TOP DELECTABLE KETOGENIC DIET RECIPES FOR A SIMPLE START! 7
   Delectable Keto Breakfast recipe 9
      Ham Cheddar Chive Soufflé 9
      Savory Sage and Cheddar Waffles 11
      Keto White Pizza Frittata 12
      Low Carb Mock McGriddle Casserole 14
      Keto Breakfast Tacos 16
      Breakfast Keto Pizza Waffles 18
      Bacon Cheddar Chive Omelets 20
      Bacon Avocado Muffins 21
      Raspberry Brie Grilled Waffles 23
      Pumpkin Spiced French Toast 25
      BBQ Pulled Pork and "Cornbread" Waffles 26
      Blueberry Banana Bread Smoothie 28
      Chicharrones con Huevos 29
      Jalapeno Cheddar Waffles 30
      Keto Zucchini Bread with Walnuts 31
      Spinach and Cheddar Scrambled Eggs 32
   Delectable Keto Dessert recipes 33
      Keto Pumpkin Snickerdoodle Cookies 33
      Easy Keto Strawberry Shortcakes 35
      Vanilla Cream Cheese Frosting 37
      Chai Spice Mug Cake 38
      Italian Lemon Sponge Cake 40

Low Carb Cookie Butter 42

LC Peanut Butter Meringue Cookies 44

Lemon & Rosemary Low Carb Shortbread 45

Coconut Peanut Butter Balls 47

Keto Cream Cheese Truffles 48

Raspberry Pavlovas 49

Keto Amaretti Cookies 51

No Bake Coconut Cashew Bars 52

Raspberry Cheesecake Cupcakes 53

Delicious Chocolate Keto Brownies 54

Baconscotch Chocolate Chunk Cookies 56

White Chocolate Bark with A Twist 58

Low Carb Spice Cakes 60

Delectable Keto Dinner Recipes 62

Chicken Zoodles 62

Ham and Cheese Bake 64

Cheddar Bacon Explosion 66

General Tso's Chicken 68

Drunken Five Spice Beef 70

Creamy Spinach Pork Tenderloin Roulade 72

Keto Paprika Chicken 74

Low Carb Chicken Satay 75

Baked Sea Bass with Herb Cauliflower Salad 77

Spicy Cauliflower Rice & Salmon Medley 79

Low Carb Sweet and Sour Meatballs 81

Hasselback Marinara Chicken 83

Low Carb Sweet and Sour Meatballs 85

Savory Italian Egg Bake 87

Skillet Browned Chicken with Creamy Greens 88

Spicy Sausage & Cabbage Skillet Melt 90

Reverse Seared Ribeye Steak 91

Keto Tater Tot Nachos (AKA Totchos) 92

Blackberry Chipotle Chicken Wings 93

Keto Chicken Pad Thai 94

Hearty Crock Pot Chicken Stew 96

40 Minute Fresh Keto Chili 98

Delectable Keto Snacks Recipes 100

Cheesy Cauliflower Onion Dip 100

Pesto Keto Crackers 101

Neopolitan Fat Bombs 102

Coconut Orange Creamsicle Fat Bombs 103

Savory Pizza Fat Bombs 104

No Bake Chocolate Peanut Butter Fat Bombs 105

Smoked Salmon and Goat Cheese Bites 106

Feta and Bacon Bites 108

Feta and Bacon Bites 110

Spicy Sausage Cheese Dip 112

Jalapeno Popper Fat Bombs 113

Keto Corndog Muffins 114

Keto Tropical Smoothie 116

Cucumber Spinach Smoothie 117

Layered Fried Queso Blanco 118

Maple Pecan Fat Bomb Bars 119

Delectable Keto Lunch Recipes 120

Savory Italian Egg Bake 120

Sausage and Kale Soup 122

Broccoli Chicken Zucchini Boats 124

Keto Mug Lasagna 126

Salmon Patties with Fresh Herbs 127
Conclusion 129

INTRODUCTION:

The 21-Day Keto-Reset.

Let be honest here, I don't know who we think we are fooling when we think we can get away with eating crappy food, or eating too much food, just because no one sees us. So I urge you to Quit "acting" healthy and BE "healthy" if you really want to get results this year. It is time to be honest with yourself and deal with your food demons. It is time to clean up and make your food as lean and healthy as you want to look

Nevertheless, life is more than just eating. I want you to view food as a way to fuel your body so that you can feel good, look good, and live your life to the fullest.

The *Keto-Reset Diet* is a lifestyle and with anything in life we hit bumps in the road. In the beginning it may be tough to keep up, but NEVER give up, keep paddling.

Eating right does wonders for your body and some of the benefits include leaner body composition, lower cholesterol and blood pressure, higher energy levels, and lower frequency of sickness.

However, discipline is far from easy but if you master the power of will and have a relentless attitude, I promise you will see many rewards. I advise you always hold yourself accountable to the best of your ability and you will never have any regrets.

Remember your body does not have the ability to turn garbage into a high quality product. Your cells, muscles, skin, bones, etc. are built by the food that you supply. So I urge you to choose wisely.

Remember, if you treat your body right it will treat you right. Time tells, in the long run your body will either be your best friend or your own worst enemy. The decision is all up to you to make!

Finally, try to get control of your eating this year, – so you can get control over your body.

The Keto-Reset Diet will keep you satisfied, clear your mind, and leave you several pounds lighter.

So "LET THE SHREDDERS BEGIN"

THE TOP DELECTABLE KETO DIET RECIPES FOR A SIMPLE START!

Delectable Keto Breakfast recipe

Ham Cheddar Chive Soufflé

Nutritional value:

NOTE: This makes a total of 5 servings.

Each serving

404 Calories

39.6g Fats

3.5g Net Carbs

19.6g Protein.

Ingredients:

½ medium Onion (diced)

6 oz. Ham Steak (cooked and cubed)

6 large Eggs

1 cup of Cheddar Cheese (shredded)

2-3 tablespoons of Fresh Chives (chopped)

¼ teaspoon of Black Pepper

3 tablespoons of Olive Oil

1 ½ teaspoons of Garlic (minced)

1 tablespoon of Butter (to grease ramekins)

½ cup of Heavy Cream

½ teaspoon of Kosher Salt

Directions:

1. Meanwhile, you heat oven to 400F.
2. After which you heat olive oil in a pan and add onions.
3. Then, once soft, add garlic to brown.
4. Add all of the ingredients together in a bowl and mix well.
5. After that, you separate mixture into ramekins and bake for 20 minutes.
6. Finally, let cool slightly and serve.

Savory Sage and Cheddar Waffles

Ingredients:

3 teaspoons of baking powder

½ teaspoon of salt

2 cups of canned coconut milk

2 eggs

1 cup of shredded cheddar cheese

1 1/3 cup of coconut flour (sifted)

1 teaspoon of dried ground sage

¼ teaspoon of garlic powder

½ cup of water

3 Tablespoons of coconut oil (melted)

Directions:

1. First, you heat your waffle iron according to manufacturer's directions, at a moderate heat.
2. After which in a mixing bowl whisk together flour, baking powder, and seasonings.
3. After that, you add liquid ingredients, then stir until stiff batter forms.
4. Then you mix in the cheese.
5. At this point, you liberally grease top and bottom panels of the waffle iron, then place a 1/3-cup scoop of batter onto each iron section.
6. This is when you close the iron and cook until steam rises from the machine and the top panel opens freely without sticking to the waffle. (NOTE: proper cooking usually takes 2 cycles at moderate heat.)

Keto White Pizza Frittata

Nutritional value:

Note: this makes a total of 8 servings of Keto White Pizza Frittata.

Each serving

298 Calories

23.8g Fats

2.1g Net Carbs

19.4g Protein.

Ingredients:

9oz bag of Frozen Spinach

5 oz. of Mozzarella Cheese

½ cup of Fresh Ricotta Cheese

4 tablespoons of Olive Oil

Salt and Pepper (to Taste)

12 large Eggs

1 oz. of Pepperoni

1 teaspoon of Minced Garlic

½ cup of Parmesan Cheese

¼ teaspoon of Nutmeg

Directions:

1. First, you microwave frozen spinach for 3-4 minutes.
2. After which you squeeze the spinach with your hands and drain off as much water as you can; set aside.
3. Meanwhile, you heat oven to 375F.
4. After that, you mix together all of the eggs, olive oil, and spices.
5. Then add in the ricotta, parmesan, and spinach. (NOTE: when adding the spinach, break it apart into small pieces.)

6. At this point, you pour the mixture into a cast iron skillet, then sprinkle mozzarella cheese over the top.
7. This is when you add pepperoni on top of that.
8. Finally, you bake for 30 minutes. Remove from the oven, slice, and serve!

Low Carb Mock McGriddle Casserole

Nutritional value:

Note: this makes a total of 8 servings of Low Carb Mock Casserole.

Each serving

482 Calories

41.4g Fats

2.9g Net Carbs

22.6g Protein.

Ingredients:

¼ cup of Flaxseed Meal

10 large Eggs

6 tablespoons of Walden Farms Maple Syrup

½ teaspoon of Onion Powder

Salt and Pepper (to Taste)

1 cup of Almond Flour

1 lb. Breakfast Sausage

4 oz. Cheese

4 tablespoons of Butter

½ teaspoon of Garlic Powder

¼ teaspoon of Sage

Directions:

1. Meanwhile, you heat oven to 350F.
2. After which you put a pan on the stove over medium heat, then add the breakfast sausage. (**NOTE:** break up while it's cooking.)
3. Then, in a separate bowl, measure out all dry ingredients (including cheese), then add the wet ingredients.

4. After that, you add 4 tablespoons of syrup and mix together well.
5. Furthermore, once the sausage is browned and somewhat crispy, add everything (including excess fat) into the mixture and mix again.
6. After which you line a 9x9 casserole dish with parchment paper and then pour the casserole mixture into the dish.
7. At this point, you use 2 tablespoons syrup drizzled over the top for extra maple flavor.
8. This is when you place in the oven and bake for 45-55 minutes.
9. Then, once done, remove from the oven and let cool.
10. Finally, you remove the casserole by holding on to the edges of the parchment paper and lifting out.

Keto Breakfast Tacos

Nutritional value:

Note: this makes a total of 3 Keto Breakfast Tacos.

Each taco

443 Calories

36.2g Fats

3g Net Carbs

25.7g Protein.

Ingredients:

6 large Eggs

3 strips of Bacon

Salt and Pepper (to Taste)

1 cup Mozzarella Cheese (shredded)

2 tablespoons of Butter

½ small Avocado

1 oz. Cheddar Cheese (shredded)

Directions:

1. First, you cook the bacon on a baking sheet with foil for about 15-20 minutes at 375F.
2. Then, while the bacon is cooking, heat 1/3 cup of mozzarella at a time on clean pan on medium heat for the shells.
3. After which you wait until the cheese is browned on the edges (about 2-3 minutes).
4. After that, you use a pair of tongs to lift the shell up and drape it over a wooden spoon resting on a pot. (NOTE: do the same with the rest of your cheese, working in batches of 1/3 cups.)
5. At this point, you cook your eggs in the butter, stirring occasionally until they're done.

6. This is when you season with salt and pepper.
7. Furthermore, you spoon a third of your scrambled eggs, avocado, and bacon into each hardened taco shell.
8. After which you sprinkle cheddar cheese over the tops of the breakfast tacos.
9. Finally, you add hot sauce and cilantro if you'd like!

Breakfast Keto Pizza Waffles

Nutritional value:

Note: this makes a total of 2 Breakfast Keto Pizza Waffles.

Each pizza waffle

526 Calories

41.5g Fats

5g Net Carbs

29g Protein.

Ingredients:

4 tablespoons of Parmesan Cheese

1 tablespoon of Psyllium Husk Powder

1 teaspoon of Baking Powder

Salt and Pepper (to Taste)

3 oz. of Cheddar Cheese

4 large Eggs

3 tablespoons of Almond Flour

1 tablespoon of Bacon Grease (or Butter)

1 teaspoon of Italian Seasoning (or spices of choice)

½ cup of Tomato Sauce (I prefer Rao's)

Pepperoni (it is optional)

Directions:

1. First, immersion blend all ingredients (except for tomato sauce and cheese) together until it thickens.
2. After which you heat your waffle iron and add half of the mixture.
3. After that, you cook until finished, then repeat.

4. Then you add tomato sauce (1/4 cup per waffle), and cheese (about 1.5 oz. per waffle) on the top of each waffle.
5. Finally, you broil for 3-5 minutes in the oven. (NOTE: Optionally add pepperoni to the top of these.)

Bacon Cheddar Chive Omelets

Nutritional value:

NOTE: makes 1 serving of Bacon Cheddar Chive Omelets.

463 Calories

39g Fats

1g Net Carbs

24g Protein

Ingredients:

1 teaspoon of Bacon Fat

1 oz. of Cheddar Cheese

Salt and Pepper (to Taste)

2 slices Bacon (already cooked)

2 large Eggs

2 stalks Chives

Directions:
1. First, you make sure all ingredients are prepped.
2. After which you heat a pan on medium-low with bacon fat in.
3. After that, you add the eggs, and season with chives, salt, and pepper.
4. Then, once the edges are starting to set, add your bacon to the center and let cook for about 20-30 seconds.
5. This is when you turn off the stove.
6. Finally, you add the cheese on top of the bacon and fold edges on top of the cheese like a burrito - holding the edges in place to use the cheese as a "glue".
7. Then you flip over and warm through on the other side.

Bacon Avocado Muffins

NOTE: this makes a total of 16 Avocado Bacon Muffins.

Per muffin

163 Calories

14.1g Fats

1.5g Net Carbs

6.1g Protein.

Ingredients:

5 Slices of Bacon

½ cup of Almond Flour

1 ½ tablespoons of Psyllium Husk Powder

4.5 oz. of Colby Jack Cheese

1 teaspoon of Minced Garlic

1 teaspoon of Dried Chives

Salt and Pepper (to Taste)

1 teaspoon of Baking Powder

5 large Eggs

2 tablespoons of Butter

¼ cup of Flaxseed Meal

2 medium Avocados

3 medium Spring Onions

1 teaspoon of Dried Cilantro

¼ teaspoon of Red Chili Flakes

1 ½ cup of coconut Milk (from the carton)

1 ½ tablespoons of Lemon Juice

Directions:

1. First, in a bowl, mix together eggs, almond flour, spices, flax, psyllium, coconut milk and lemon juice.
2. After which you leave to sit while you cook the bacon.
3. Then in a pan over medium-low heat, cook the bacon until crisp.
4. After that, you add the butter to the pan when it's almost done the cooking.
5. You chop the spring onions and grate the cheese.
6. At this point, you add the spring onions, cheese, and baking powder; crumble the bacon.
7. This is when you add the crumbled bacon and melted butter to the batter.
8. Furthermore, slice an avocado in half, remove the pit, and then cube the avocado while it's in the shell. (NOTE: Be careful of the sharp knife as you do this.)
9. After that, you scoop out the avocado and fold into the mixture gently.
10. Meanwhile, you heat oven to 350F, measure out batter into a cupcake tray that's been sprayed or greased and bake for about 24-26 minutes. (NOTE: you should have a leftover batter to make 4 more muffins, which you Store in the fridge and enjoy cold!)

Raspberry Brie Grilled Waffles

Nutritive value:

NOTE: this makes 2 servings of Raspberry Brie Grilled Waffles.

Each serving

489 Calories

39.5g Fats

7g Net Carbs

21g Protein.

Ingredients:

The Waffles

2 tablespoons of flaxseed meal

1 teaspoon of Vanilla Extract

2 large Eggs

7 drops of liquid Stevia

½ cup Almond Flour

1/3 cup of Coconut Milk

1 teaspoon of Baking Powder

2 tablespoons of Swerve

The Filling

Zest of ½ Lemon

2 tablespoons of Butter

3 oz. of Double Cream Brie

½ cup of Raspberries

1 tablespoon of Lemon Juice

1 tablespoon of Swerve

Directions:

1. First, you mix together all waffle ingredients and then cook on a waffle iron.
2. Then, while warm, lay slices of brie across waffles.
3. After which in a pan, heat butter and swerve.
4. Once browning, you add raspberries and lemon juice/zest.
5. After that, you let this cook until bubbling and jam-like.
6. At this point, you place waffle sides with brie under a broiler until brie is soft and waffle is slightly crisp.
7. Finally, you assemble waffle with brie and raspberry compote.
8. Then you "Grill" in a pan over medium heat for 1-2 minutes per side.

Pumpkin Spiced French Toast

Nutritive value:

Note: this makes a total of 2 servings.

Each serving

428 Calories

37.4g Fats

6.8g Net Carbs

12g Protein.

Ingredients:

1 large Egg

½ teaspoon of Vanilla Extract

2 tablespoons of Butter

4 slices of Pumpkin Bread

2 tablespoons of Cream

1/8 teaspoon of Orange Extract

¼ teaspoon of Pumpkin Pie Spice

Directions:

1. First, you let the bread dry out overnight in open air after you have sliced it.
2. After which you mix together egg, extracts, and pumpkin pie spice.
3. After that, you let the bread soak on both sides in the mixture.
4. Then you heat butter in a pan until almost browned, then add bread slices.
5. This is when you flip when browned and continue to cook until browned on both sides.
6. Finally, you serve with Keto maple syrup and some extra powdered swerve.

BBQ Pulled Pork and "Cornbread" Waffles

Nutritive value:

NOTE: this makes 4 total servings of 1 waffle and 4oz. of pulled pork.

Each serving

556 Calories

45.3g Fats

5.7g Net Carbs

26.4g Protein.

Ingredients:

1 cup of Almond Flour

½ teaspoon of Salt

2 tablespoons of Butter

2 tablespoons of Golden Flaxseed Meal

¼ cup of Coconut Milk (from carton)

¼ cup of BBQ Sauce

16 oz. of Pulled Pork

1 teaspoon of Baking Powder

3 large Eggs

¼ cup of Sour Cream

1 tablespoon of Psyllium Husk

2 tablespoons of Chopped Red Pepper

Directions:

1. First, you make the BBQ Sauce and then make the waffle batter by mixing the wet ingredients into the dry.
2. After which you pour the batter on to the waffle maker and let cook.
3. Then, while cooking, add pork to a pan on medium-low heat with about 3/4 of the BBQ sauce.

4. Finally, once waffles are done, spoon pork onto waffle and top with extra bbq sauce.
5. Make sure you serve with extra sour cream if you'd like!

Blueberry Banana Bread Smoothie

Nutritive value:

NOTE: this makes 2 total servings of Blueberry Banana Bread Shake.

Per serving

264 Calories

25g Fats

3g Net Carbs

4g Protein.

Ingredients:

3 tablespoons of Golden Flaxseed Meal

1 tablespoon of Chia Seeds

2 cups of Vanilla Unsweetened Coconut Milk

10 drop of Liquid Stevia

¼ cup of Blueberries

2 tablespoons of MCT oil

1 ½ teaspoons of Banana Extract

¼ teaspoon of Xanthan Gum

Directions:

1. First, you add all ingredients together into a blender. (for me, I prefer to wait a few minutes so that the flax and chia seeds have enough time to soak up some of the moisture.)
2. Then you blend for 1-2 minutes until everything is incorporated well; serve up!

THE KETO-RESET DIET COOKBOOK

Chicharrones con Huevos

Nutritive value:

NOTE: this makes 3 total servings of Chicharrones con Huevos.

Each serving

508 Calories

43g Fats

5g Net Carbs

24.7g Protein.

Ingredients:

5 large Eggs

1 medium Tomato

2 medium Jalapeno Peppers (de-seeded)

Salt and Pepper (to Taste)

4 slices of Bacon

1.5 oz. of Pork Rinds

1 medium Avocado

¼ medium Onion

¼ cup of Cilantro (chopped)

Directions:

1. First, you cook bacon and remove to paper towels for later.
2. After which you keep bacon fat in the pan.
3. After that, you cook pork rinds in bacon fat, then add diced vegetables.
4. Then, once onions are almost translucent, add cilantro and mix together.
5. At this point, you add pre-scrambled eggs, let cook, and stir once.
6. Finally, cube and avocado and fold into the eggs.
7. Enjoy!

Jalapeno Cheddar Waffles

Nutritional value:

Note: this makes a total of 2 Jalapeno Cheddar Waffles.

Each waffle

338 Calories

28g Fats

3g Net Carbs

16g Protein.

Ingredients:

3 large Eggs

1 teaspoon of Psyllium Husk Powder

1 oz. of Cheddar Cheese

Salt and Pepper (to Taste)

3 oz. of Cream Cheese

1 tablespoon of Coconut Flour

1 teaspoon of Baking Powder

1 small Jalapeno

Directions:

1. First, you mix together all ingredients using an immersion blender, until everything is smooth.
2. After which you heat your waffle iron, then pour in the waffle mix. (NOTE: about 5-6 minutes in total.)
3. Finally, you top with your favorite toppings, and serve!

Keto Zucchini Bread with Walnuts

Ingredients:

½ cup of olive oil

2 ½ cups of almond flour

½ teaspoon of salt

½ teaspoon of nutmeg

¼ teaspoon of ground ginger

½ cup of chopped walnuts

3 large eggs

1 teaspoon of vanilla extract

1 ½ cups of erythritol

1 ½ teaspoons of baking powder

1 teaspoon of ground cinnamon

1 cup of grated zucchini

Directions:

1. Meanwhile, you heat oven to 350°F.
2. After which you whisk together the eggs, oil, and vanilla extract; set to the side.
3. Then in another bowl, mix together the almond flour, baking powder, nutmeg, erythritol, salt, cinnamon, and ginger; Set to the side.
4. After that, use a cheesecloth or paper towel, take the zucchini and squeeze out the excess water.
5. At this point, you whisk the zucchini into the bowl with the eggs.
6. Furthermore, you slowly add the dry ingredients into the egg mixture using a hand mixer until fully blended.
7. After which you lightly spray a 9x5 loaf pan, and spoon in the zucchini bread mixture.
8. This is when you spoon in the chopped walnuts on top of the zucchini bread.
9. After that, you press walnuts into the batter using a spatula.
10. Finally, you bake for 60-70 minutes at 350°F or until the walnuts on top look browned.

Spinach and Cheddar Scrambled Eggs

Nutritional value:

One serving:

698 calories

57g fat

6g carb

3g fiber (3g net carb)

40g protein

Ingredients:

4 Cups of Fresh Spinach

1 Tablespoon of Olive Oil

Pinch Pepper

4 Large Eggs

½ Cup of Cheddar Cheese

1 Tablespoon of Heavy Cream

Pinch Salt

Directions:

1. First, you assemble ingredients together.
2. After which you add your 4 eggs to a cup or bowl.
3. After that, you add 1 tablespoon of heavy cream and salt and pepper to taste.
4. Make sure you mix so there are still egg whites showing.
5. Then you heat a large pan to high with 1tablespoon olive oil
6. At this point, you add your spinach once the oil has reached its smoke point.
7. Furthermore, you add salt and pepper as the spinach begins to sizzle, stirring frequently.
8. Then once the spinach has fully wilted, reduce heat to medium low and add eggs.
9. Finally, you stir slowly once the eggs have set and add your cheese.
10. Once it melted, then you plate and enjoy!

Delectable Keto Dessert recipes

Keto Pumpkin Snickerdoodle Cookies

Nutritional value:

Note: this makes a total of 15 Keto Pumpkin Snickerdoodle Cookies.

Per cookie

104.53 Calories

9.4g Fats

1.5g Net Carbs

2.99g Protein.

Ingredients:

The Cookies

¼ cup of Butter (salted)

1 teaspoon of Vanilla Extract

1 large Egg

25 drops of Liquid Stevia

1 ½ cups of Almond Flour

½ cup of Pumpkin Puree

½ teaspoon of Baking Powder

¼ cup of Erythritol

The Topping:

2 teaspoons of Erythritol

1 teaspoon of Pumpkin Pie Spice

Directions:

1. Meanwhile, you heat oven to 350F.
2. After which you measure out dry ingredients and mix.
3. Then in a separate container, you measure out the butter, pumpkin puree, vanilla, and liquid stevia.
4. At this point, you mix everything together well until a pastry dough is formed.
5. After that, you roll the dough into small balls and set on a cookie sheet covered with a Silpat. (NOTE: About 15 cookies in total.)
6. Furthermore, you press the balls flat with your hand (or the bottom side of a jar) and bake for about 12-13 minutes.
7. Finally, while the cookies are cooking, run 2 teaspoons of erythritol and 1 teaspoon of pumpkin pie spice through a spice grinder.
8. Once the cookies are done, I suggest you sprinkle with the topping and let cool completely.

Easy Keto Strawberry Shortcakes

Nutritional value:

Note: this makes a total of 5 Keto Strawberry Shortcakes.

Per shortcake

273.2 Calories

25.96g Fats

3.94g Net Carbs

6.64g Protein.

Ingredients:

Keto Puff Cakes

3 oz. of Cream Cheese

2 tablespoons of Erythritol

3 large Eggs

¼ teaspoon of Baking Powder

½ teaspoon of Vanilla Extract

Filling

1 cup of Heavy Cream

10 medium Strawberries

Directions:
1. Meanwhile, you heat oven to 300F.
2. After which you separate the egg whites from the yolks.
3. After that, start by beating the egg whites until they are fluffy.
4. Then in the container with the yolks, add cream cheese, vanilla, baking powder, and erythritol and beat until smooth.
5. At this point, you fold egg whites slowly into the egg yolk mixture, then spread evenly on a baking sheet with a Silpat.
6. Finally, you bake for about 25-30 minutes.

7. This is when you let cool, then sandwich whipped cream and strawberries between 2 cakes.

Vanilla Cream Cheese Frosting

Ingredients:

¼ cup of powdered erythritol

½ teaspoon of vanilla extract

4 ounces of cream cheese

3 tablespoons of heavy whipping cream

Directions:

1. Meanwhile, you heat oven to 350° F while gathering your ingredients.
2. After which, in a medium sized bowl, mix the eggs, mayonnaise, and vanilla bean paste.
3. If you want the batter to be really smooth, I suggest you use a hand mixer.
4. After that, you set the bowl to the side.
5. Then in another bowl, mix together the almond flour, erythritol, salt, and baking powder.
6. At this point, you slowly whisk the batter into the almond flour. (NOTE: if you have a hard time mixing them together, I suggest you use the hand blender until it is smooth.)
7. However, the mixture will seem a little dry when it's mixed, but this is normal.
8. Furthermore, using a ¼ cup measure, spoon out eight servings into a lined muffin or cupcake pan.
9. Finally, you bake for 20-25 minutes at 350° F or until they're lightly browned on top.
10. Make sure you frost after they have cooled.

Chai Spice Mug Cake

Nutritional value: Per cake

447 Calories

41.94g Fats

4.97g Net Carbs

12.67g Protein.

Ingredients:

Base

2 tablespoons of butter

1 tablespoon of erythritol

½ teaspoon of baking powder

1 large egg

2 tablespoons of almond flour

7 drops of liquid Stevia

Flavor

¼ teaspoon of cinnamon

¼ teaspoon of clove

¼ teaspoon of vanilla extract

2 tablespoons of almond flour

¼ teaspoon of ginger

¼ teaspoon of cardamom

Directions:

1. First, you mix all room temperature ingredients together in a mug.
2. After which you microwave on high for 70 seconds.

3. After that, you turn the cup upside down and lightly bang it against a plate.
4. **Optional:** feel free to top with whipped cream and sprinkle of cinnamon.

Italian Lemon Sponge Cake

Nutritional value:

Note: this made a total of 3 cakes.

Each cake

414 Calories

38g Fats

5.4g Net Carbs

18g Protein.

With the icing:

634 Calories

58.26g Fats

7.11g Net Carbs

19.39g Protein.

Cut the cakes into halves or make them in a cupcake for easy serving!

Ingredients:

Italian Sponge Cake

1 teaspoon of Baking Powder

5 large Eggs (Separated)

1 teaspoon of Almond Extract

¼ teaspoon of Liquid Stevia

½ teaspoon of Cream of Tartar (for egg whites)

1 cup of Honey Ville Almond Flour

¼ teaspoon of Salt

1 teaspoon of Vanilla

¼ cup of NOW Erythritol

Zest ½ Lemon

2 tablespoons of Olive Oil

Raspberry Lemon Icing

Ingredients:

4 tablespoons of Heavy Cream

Juice ½ Lemon

4 tablespoons of Butter

1/3 cup of Fresh Raspberries

Directions:

1. Meanwhile, you heat oven to 325F.
2. After which you mix all dry ingredients together (EXCEPT cream of tartar), then mix all wet ingredients together (EXCEPT egg whites and lemon zest).
3. After that, you whip egg whites in a small mixing bowl with the cream of tartar and lemon zest until still peaks form.
4. Then you aggressively fold 1/3 egg white mixture into batter.
5. This is when you add the rest and gently fold it in.
6. At this point, you pour batter among cupcake molds or cake molds and bake for 25 minutes.
7. Then, while the cake is cooking, heat butter until it starts to brown.
8. Add cream and lemon juice and remove from heat while you continue stirring.
9. After which you add raspberries and lightly mash with a fork into the frosting.
10. Let cool for about10-15 minutes.
11. Finally, ice cake and serve!

Low Carb Cookie Butter

Nutritional value:

Note: this makes about 1 cup of Low Carb Cookie Butter.

Each tablespoon

117.25 Calories

11.45g Fats

2.46g Net Carbs

1.72g Protein.

Ingredients:

¾ cup of Raw Cashews

¼ teaspoon of Cinnamon

1/8 teaspoon of Nutmeg

2 tablespoons of Butter

Pinch Salt

1 cup of Raw Macadamias

1 teaspoon of Vanilla

¼ teaspoon of Ginger

1/8 teaspoon of Cloves

2 tablespoons of Heavy Cream

2 tablespoons of Swerve (powdered)

Directions:

1. First, you add macadamia nuts and cashews into food processor and process until smooth.
2. After which you brown the butter with the powdered Swerve in a saucepan.
3. Then once butter is brown, add heavy cream and stir into the butter.
4. After that, you remove from heat.

5. At this point, you add vanilla and spices, then process again until well combined and little to no lumps inside.

NOTE: While processing, pour in caramel sauce and continue the process until you're happy with the consistency.

THE KETO-RESET DIET COOKBOOK

LC Peanut Butter Meringue Cookies

Nutritional value: this makes a total of 18 servings of Peanut Butter Meringue Cookies.

Each serving

49.83 Calories

3.7g Fats

1.34g Net Carbs

3.06g Protein.

Ingredients:

2 tablespoons of sweetener

1 cup of egg whites (room temp)

½ cup of creamy peanut butter

Directions:

1. Meanwhile, you heat oven to 200°F.
2. After which you beat egg whites on high speed till soft peaks form.
3. After that, you turn the speed down and while beating slowly add sweetener.
4. Then you add peanut butter and mix on low speed till combined.
5. At this point, you place 2 Tablespoons of meringue on parchment- or Silpat-covered baking sheet.
6. After that, you bake for 1 hour without opening the oven door.
7. Finally, you turn oven off and leave cookies in the oven for an additional hour.

Lemon & Rosemary Low Carb Shortbread

Nutritional value:

Note: this makes a total of 24 servings of Lemon & Rosemary Low Carb Shortbread.

Each serving

79.92 Calories

7.56g Fats

1.14g Net Carbs

2.04g Protein.

Ingredients:

2 cups of almond flour

1 tablespoon of freshly grated lemon zest

1 teaspoon of vanilla extract

½ teaspoon of baking powder

6 tablespoons of butter

1/3 cup of granulated Splenda (or better still another granulated sweetener)

4 teaspoons of squeezed lemon juice

2 teaspoons of rosemary

½ teaspoon of baking soda

Directions:
1. First, you measure out 2 cups of almond flour, ½ teaspoon baking powder, and ½ teaspoon baking soda in a large mixing bowl.
2. After which you add 1/3 cup Splenda or another granulated sweetener to the mixture; set aside.
3. After that, you zest your lemon with a micro plane until you have 1 Tablespoon of lemon zest. (NOTE: Juice half the lemon to get 4teaspoon lemon juice.)

4. Then in the microwave, melt 6 Tablespoons of butter and then add 1 teaspoon vanilla extract.
5. At this point, you transfer your almond flour and sweetener to a small mixing bowl.
6. After that, you put your butter, lemon zest, lemon juice, and chopped rosemary into the now empty large mixing bowl.
7. After which you add your almond flour back into the wet mixture slowly, stirring as you go.
8. Make sure you keep mixing until all the almond flour is added back.
9. This is when you wrap the dough tightly in plastic wrap.
10. Furthermore, you place the wrapped dough in the freezer for 30 minutes, or until hard.
11. Meanwhile, you heat your oven to 350F, remove your dough, and unwrap it.
12. After which you cut your dough in ~1/2" increments with a sharp knife. NOTE: If this knife isn't sharp, it will make the dough crumble. If the dough is still crumbling, it implies that it needs more time in the freezer.
13. Then you grease a cookie sheet with SALTED butter and place your cookies on it.
14. Finally, you bake for about 15 minutes at 350 degrees.
15. Once removed, I suggest you allow to cool for 10 minutes, remove from cookie sheet, and enjoy!

Notes

For me; I used dried rosemary, but fresh would be even better.

Coconut Peanut Butter Balls

Ingredients:

3 teaspoons of unsweetened cocoa powder

½ cup of unsweetened coconut flakes

3 tablespoons of creamy peanut butter

2 ½ teaspoons of powdered erythritol

2 teaspoons of almond flour

Directions:

1. First, you mix together your peanut butter, cocoa, erythritol, and flour, in a bowl.
2. After which you freeze for one hour.
3. Using a melon baller (or better still small spoon), spoon out a small serving of the peanut butter mix.
4. After that, you drop it into your coconut flakes and roll around with your hands so the coconut covers the ball. (NOTE: Reshape into a ball if needed.)
5. Finally, you refrigerate overnight so they firm up.

Keto Cream Cheese Truffles

Ingredients:

½ cup of unsweetened cocoa powder (divided)

¼ teaspoon of liquid Stevia

1 tablespoon of instant coffee

24 paper candy cups (for serving)

16 ounces' cream cheese (softened)

4 tablespoons of Swerve confectioners

½ teaspoon of rum extract

2 tablespoons of water

1 tablespoon of heavy whipping cream

Directions:

1. First, in a large bowl add the cream cheese, ¼ cup of cocoa powder, rum extract, instant coffee, Swerve, Stevia, water, and heavy whipping cream.
2. After which you use an electric hand mixer to whip all of the ingredients together until they are well combined.
3. After that, you place the bowl in the fridge for half an hour to chill before rolling.
4. Then you spread the remaining ¼ cup cocoa powder out.
5. At this point, you roll heaping tablespoons in the palm of your hand to form balls, then roll them around in the cocoa powder. (NOTE: You will end up with about 24 total.)
6. Finally, you place them individually in small paper candy cups.
7. Make sure you chill for an hour before serving.

Raspberry Pavlovas

Ingredients:

Base:

½ cup of Erythritol

2 teaspoons of Xanthan Gum

4 large Egg Whites

1 teaspoon of Vanilla Extract

1 teaspoon of Fresh Lemon Juice

Filling:

85g Frozen Berries

1 cup of heavy cream

Topping:

18 Fresh Raspberries

1-2 Mint Leaves

Directions:

1. Meanwhile, you heat oven to 300°F.
2. After which you separate 4 eggs carefully and beat the egg whites until they're foamy.
3. After that, you add in erythritol a little at a time while beating.
4. At this point, you mix until stiff peaks.
5. Then you add in vanilla, lemon juice, and xanthan gum; then fold together with a silicone spatula.
6. Furthermore, you line a baking sheet with parchment paper and use a pencil to outline a cup or bowl to guide you when spooning the pavlova mixture. (NOTE: This recipe makes 6 mini pavlovas about 5 inches in diameter.)
7. After which you spoon the pavlova batter so that it's roughly the size of each circle you've drawn.

8. Using the back of a spoon, create a dip/well in the center for the filling later, then you bake for an hour. (NOTE: The pavlovas should turn a crisp, golden brown.)
9. At this point, while the pavlovas are cooling, I suggest you prepare the filling.
10. Measure out 85g of mixed frozen berries (NOTE: Strawberries, blueberries, and blackberries work well to make a beautiful purple color.)
11. This is the point when you blend with a cup of heavy cream for about 3 minutes so the mixture is thick enough to spoon.
12. Finally, you spoon some of the frozen berry mixtures into each pavlova and top with some fresh berries and mint!

Keto Amaretti Cookies

Ingredients:

2 tablespoons of Coconut Flour

¼ teaspoon of Cinnamon

½ cup of Erythritol

4 tablespoons of Coconut Oil

½ teaspoon of Almond Extract

1 tablespoon of Shredded Coconut

1 cup of Almond Flour

½ teaspoon of Baking Powder

½ teaspoon of Salt

2 large Eggs

½ teaspoon of Vanilla Extract

2 tablespoons of Sugar-Free Jam

Directions:

1. Meanwhile, you heat your oven to 350F.
2. After which you combine all your dry ingredients, then add wet ingredients and combine well.
3. After that, you form your cookies on a parchment paper lined baking sheet.
4. Then you add an indent in the middle of each cookie using your finger.
5. This is when you bake for about 16 minutes or until the cookies turn golden and crack slightly.
6. After which you let cookies cool on a wire rack and add a bit of sugar-free jam to each indent.
7. Finally, you sprinkle some shredded coconut on top of each one and enjoy!

No Bake Coconut Cashew Bars

Nutritional value:

Note: this makes a total of 8 servings of No Bake Coconut Cashew Bars.

Each serving

197.36 Calories

18.39g Fats

4.45g Net Carbs

4.55g Protein.

Ingredients:

¼ cup of Butter (melted)

1 teaspoon of Cinnamon

¼ cup of Shredded Coconut

1 cup of Almond Flour

¼ cup of Sugar-Free Maple Syrup (like Walden's Farms or make your own)

1 pinch of Salt

½ cup of Cashews

Directions:

1. First, you combine melted butter and almond flour in a large bowl and combine.
2. After which you add cinnamon, salt, sugar-free maple syrup and shredded coconut; mix well.
3. After that, you roughly chop ½ cup of cashews (you may use raw or roasted) and add it into your coconut cashew bar dough.
4. Then you mix very well again.
5. This is when you line a baking dish with parchment paper and spread the coconut cashew bar dough in an even layer.
6. Finally, you place them in the refrigerator and chill for minimum 2 hours.
7. Once they're chilled, I suggest you slice into bars and enjoy!

Raspberry Cheesecake Cupcakes

Nutritional value:

Note: this will make 12 total servings that are fluffy and decadent.

Per serving

205.83 Calories

19.98g Fats

2.69g Net Carbs

4.41g Protein.

Ingredients:

½ cup of Almond Meal

½ cup of Granulated Sweetener (I prefer Stevia)

¼ cup of Sugar-Free Raspberry Syrup (or better still desired flavor)

½ stick (about 4 tbsp) Butter (melted)

2-8oz. of packages Cream Cheese (softened)

1 teaspoon of Vanilla

2 large eggs

Directions:

1. First, you heat your oven to 350F bake.
2. After which you grease or line a cupcake tin (you'll need 12 spots)
3. After that, you mix the melted butter in with the almond meal.
4. Then you press the almond meal mixture into the bottoms of the cupcake tins.
5. In a stand mixer, you add the cream cheese, eggs, stevia, sugar-free syrup, and vanilla to the bowl and mix on medium speed until the mixture is smooth.
6. Once the mixture is smooth, you evenly pour the mix into the cupcake tins, filling almost to the top.
7. At this point, you bake in the oven for about 15-17 minutes.
8. Finally, you let stand for 10 minutes before putting into the fridge for at least 30 minutes.

Delicious Chocolate Keto Brownies

Nutritional value:

Note: this makes a total of 6 servings of Delicious Chocolate Keto Brownies.

Each serving

196 Calories

17.68g Fats

2.7g Net Carbs

6.13g Protein.

Ingredients:

3 large eggs

2 tablespoons of cocoa powder (heaped)

¼ cup of coconut flour

9 packets Truvia

1 teaspoon of vanilla extract

Pinch of salt

6 tablespoons of cream cheese

3 tablespoons of coconut oil

¼ cup of almond flour

¼ teaspoon of baking soda

¼ - ½ cup of almond milk

Directions:

1. Meanwhile, you heat oven to 375 degrees F
2. After which you combine cream cheese, eggs, coconut oil, almond milk, and vanilla extract in one bowl; Mix well until smooth.
3. After that, you combine cocoa powder, baking soda, truvia, almond flour, coconut flour, and salt in another bowl.

4. Then you slowly add wet ingredients to dry and mix well
5. At this point, you pour batter into cake pan or brownie pan and bake for about 30 minutes (or until a toothpick comes out clean)
6. Finally, you let cool 5 minutes and cut as desired

Baconscotch Chocolate Chunk Cookies

Nutritional value:

Note: this makes a total of 24 servings of Chocolate Chunk Cookies.

Each serving

117.24 Calories

10.62g Fats

1.36g Net Carbs

3.13g Protein.

Ingredients:

3.5 ounces of unsweetened baker's chocolate

½ cup of softened butter

One large egg

½ teaspoon of vanilla extract

6 slices of candied bacon

1 ½ cups of almond flour

½ cup of erythritol

2 tablespoons of scotch

1 teaspoon of baking powder

Directions:

1. First, you mix all dry ingredients together.
2. After which you cream the butter, add the egg and vanilla and mix until creamy.
3. After that, you slowly add dry ingredients to wet ingredients.
4. At this point, you fold in 2 Oz. chopped chocolate and chopped candied bacon.
5. This is when you put the dough in the freezer for 20-30 minutes.
6. Then you roll flat and form into balls on the baking sheet.
7. Finally, you press balls flat and bake for about 20-22 minutes at 325F.

8. Make sure you top with chocolate ganache (made with 1.5 Oz Chocolate) dipped bacon and drizzled chocolate ganache.

Notes

Remember that whiskey or Bourbon can be subbed in for this, as long as it has a sweet smell.

White Chocolate Bark with A Twist

Nutritional value:

Note: this makes a total of 12 servings of White Chocolate Bark.

Each serving

23.92 Calories

2.36g Fats

0.11g Net Carbs

0.13g Protein.

Ingredients:

1/3 cup of erythritol

½ teaspoon of hemp seed powder

1 teaspoon of toasted pumpkin seeds

2 ounces of cacao butter

1 teaspoon of vanilla powder

Pinch of salt

Directions:
1. First, you measure out the 2oz cacao butter and chop finely.
2. After which you put the cacao butter in the top of a double boiler or in a bowl that can be placed over a pan of boiling water.
3. After that, you mix remaining ingredients into a separate bowl and mix well.
4. Then you turn the burner on and bring water in the pan to a low boil over medium high heat.
5. At this point, you continue cooking just until cacao butter is melted.
6. Then while cacao butter is melting, grease a small bowl or plate with butter or coconut oil. (NOTE: As soon as the cacao butter is melted, remove from heat and mix in remaining ingredients).
7. This is when you stir well and pour into the greased dish.

8. Finally, once the mixture has set, remove from dish and break into 12 equal pieces. (NOTE: To speed up this process, you can place the dish in the freezer for about 15 minutes)
9. Make sure you put them away and enjoy as a great snack!

THE KETO-RESET DIET COOKBOOK

Low Carb Spice Cakes

Nutritional value: Per cupcake

285.17 Calories

27.07g Fats

3.64g Net Carbs

7.38g Protein

Ingredients:

Spice Cakes

¾ Cup of Erythritol

5 Tablespoons of Water

2 teaspoons of Baking Powder

½ teaspoon of Cinnamon

½ teaspoon of Allspice

¼ teaspoon of Ground Clove

2 Cups of Fine Almond Flour

½ Cup of Salted Butter

4 Large Eggs

1 teaspoon of Vanilla Extract

½ teaspoon of Nutmeg

½ teaspoon of Ginger

Cream Cheese Frosting

2 Tablespoons of Butter

½ of Lemon's Zest

8 Oz. of Cream Cheese

3 Tablespoons of Erythritol

1 teaspoon of Vanilla Extract

Directions:

1. Meanwhile, you heat your oven to 350F.
2. After which in a mixing bowl, add your butter and sweetener. Make sure you cream it together until smooth.
3. After that, you add 2 of your eggs and continue mixing it until combined, then add and mix in your last 2 eggs.
4. Then you grind up your spices, then add all the dry ingredients to the batter; mix until smooth.
5. At this point, you add your water to the batter and mix well, until it is creamy.
6. This is when you spray your cupcake tray, fill it about 3/4 of the way up, and put them in the oven for 15 minutes.
7. Furthermore, while they're cooking, cream together your cream cheese, butter, sweetener, vanilla, and lemon zest for the frosting.
8. Finally, you remove your cupcakes from the oven, let them cool for 15 minutes, and then frost them.

Delectable Keto Dinner Recipes

Chicken Zoodles

Nutritional value:

Note: this makes 1 serving of Thai Chicken Zoodles.

580 Calories

49.1g Fats

6.8g Net Carbs

25.8g Protein.

Ingredients:

3.5 oz. of Chicken Thigh

1 tablespoon of Coconut Oil

1 clove of Garlic

1.4 oz. of Bean Sprouts

1 teaspoon of Soy Sauce (or better still Coconut Aminos)

1/8 teaspoon of White Pepper

Pinch of Salt and Pepper

½ teaspoon of Curry Powder

1 tablespoon of Unsalted Butter

1 stalk of Spring Onion

1 large Egg

3.5 oz. of Zucchini

½ teaspoon of Oyster Sauce

1 teaspoon of Lime Juice

Red Chilies (chopped)

Directions:

1. First, you marinate Chicken with Curry Powder and Salt and Pepper.
2. After which, you prepare the sauce by combining Oyster Sauce, Soy Sauce, and White Pepper.
3. After that, you chop finely the Spring Onion and Garlic and make Zoodles out of Zucchini.
4. At this point, you fry the Chicken with Unsalted Butter until brown; sliced to bite-sized pieces.
5. Then, with the same pan on high heat, add Coconut oil.
6. Furthermore, you sauté chopped Spring Onion until fragrant.
7. Add in chopped Garlic.
8. This is when you crack an Egg and scramble.
9. After that, you brown the egg slightly.
10. Then you add Bean Sprouts and Zoodles and mix in the sauce.
11. Make sure you thicken the sauce a bit.
12. Add in fried Chicken pieces and stir.
13. Finally, you garnish with chopped Red Chilies and squeeze Lime Juice.
14. Serve!

Ham and Cheese Bake

Nutritional value:

Per serving

646 Calories

52.8g Fats

7.1g Net Carbs

37g Protein.

Ingredients:

2 cups of Chopped Ham (preferably, pre-cooked)

½ cup of Sour Cream

1 cup of Cubed Mozzarella

½ teaspoon of Garlic Powder

2 (12oz) bags of Chopped Frozen Cauliflower

1 ½ cups of Heavy Whipping Cream

2 ½ cups of Shredded Sharp Cheddar Cheese

½ teaspoon of Black Pepper

Directions:
1. Meanwhile, you heat your oven to 375F bake.
2. After which you grease a 13x9 casserole.
3. After that, you empty the frozen cauliflower into a medium pot and cover with water.
4. Then you bring the cauliflower to a boil and cook for about 8-10 minutes until tender.
5. This is when you drain the cauliflower and return it to the pot.
6. At this point, you grab your potato masher (or food processor) and mash (or process) the cauliflower to the desired consistency.
7. Furthermore, you spread the mashed cauliflower into the bottom of the casserole dish.

8. After that, you layer the chopped ham over the cauliflower and set aside.
9. However, in a medium sauce pan, mix the shredded cheese, sour cream, heavy whipping cream, and seasonings together over medium heat until the cheese is slightly melted.
10. Then, once melted, you evenly pour the mixture over the layers of ham and cauliflower.
11. Finally, top the casserole with the cubed cheese and put in the oven to bake for about 40-45 minutes (or until the cheese on top browns).

Cheddar Bacon Explosion

Nutritional value: per serving

432 Calories

38.2g Fats

3g Net Carbs

32.8g Protein.

Ingredients:

2 ½ Cups of Cheddar Cheese

2 teaspoons of Mrs. Dash Table Seasoning

30 Slices of Bacon

4-5 Cups of Raw Spinach

1-2 Tablespoons of Tones Southwest Chipotle Seasoning

Directions:

1. Meanwhile, you heat your oven to 375F convection bake.
2. After which, weave the bacon. 15 pieces that are vertical, 12 pieces' horizontal, and the extra 3 cut in half to fill in rest, horizontally.
3. After that, you season your bacon with your favorite seasoning mix.
4. Then you add your cheese to the bacon, leaving about 1 ½ inch gaps between the edges.
5. Furthermore, add your spinach and press down on it to compress it some. (NOTE: this will help when you roll it up.)
6. After which you roll your weave slowly, making sure it stays tight and not too much falls through.
7. Remember, you may have some cheese fall out, but don't worry about it.
8. After that, you add your seasoning to the outside here.
9. Then you foil a baking sheet and add plenty of salt to it. (NOTE: this will help catch excess grease from the bacon and not let your oven smoke.)
10. At this point, you put your bacon on top of a cooling rack and put that on top of your baking sheet.

11. This is when you bake for about 60-70 minutes, without opening the oven door. (NOTE: pour bacon should be very crisp on the top when finished.)
12. Finally, you let cool for 10-15 minutes before trying to take it off the cooling rack.

Make sure you slice into pieces and serve!

General Tso's Chicken

Ingredients:

Chicken

¾ Cup of Crushed Pork Rinds

2 Large Eggs

1 Tablespoon of Coconut Oil

6-7 Small Chicken Breasts

1/3 Cup of Almond Flour

2 Tablespoons of Olive Oil

Sauce

3 Tablespoons of Rice Vinegar

2 Tablespoons of Reduced Sugar Ketchup

2 teaspoons of Sesame Oil

1 teaspoon of Red Chili Paste

1 teaspoon of Garlic Powder

¼ teaspoon of Xanthan Gum

¼ Cup of Chicken Broth

2 ½ Tablespoons of Soy Sauce

2 Tablespoons of Erythritol

1 teaspoon of Hoisin Sauce

1 teaspoon of Red Chili Flakes

½ teaspoon of Minced Ginger

Optional:

NOTE: garnish with chives, red chili pepper flakes, or red chili peppers.

Directions:

1. First, you put pork rinds in the food processor and pulse them until crushed.
2. After which you combine almond flour with pork rinds in one bowl, scramble 2 eggs in another bowl.
3. Meanwhile, you heat oven to 325F.
4. After that, you wash and cube chicken breasts.
5. Then you dip chicken in egg, dip chicken in pork rinds and almond flour.
6. Furthermore, you fry chicken in olive and coconut oil.
7. This is when you make the sauce and cover chicken with sauce.
8. Finally, you bake chicken in sauce for 1 hour, turning/mixing chicken every 15 minutes.

Notes

This recipe makes about 3 servings at 1.4 pounds each, depending on the size of chicken breasts you use. At 3 servings, you get 566 Calories, 37.3g Fats, 4.5g Net Carbs, and 59.3g Protein.

Drunken Five Spice Beef

Nutritional value:

Note: this makes 4 Total Servings

Each serving:

515 Calories

35g Fats

6g Net Carbs

33.25g Protein.

Ingredients:

1 Can Coors Light (Or better still ½ Cup Red Wine)

135g of Chopped Broccoli

3 Tablespoons of Reduced Sugar Ketchup

2 teaspoons of Garlic

2 teaspoons of Salt

½ teaspoon of Onion Powder

1 ½ lbs. of Ground Beef

150g of Sliced Mushrooms

75g of Raw Spinach

2 Tablespoons of Soy Sauce

2 teaspoons of Minced ginger

1 Tablespoon of Pepper

2 teaspoons of Cumin

1 teaspoon of Cayenne Pepper

Directions:

1. First, you chop up broccoli florets, ginger, and garlic.
2. After which you bring cast iron to high heat and add ground beef.
3. After that, you brown all ground beef then add ginger and garlic to the pan.
4. Then you mix everything well, add broccoli and spices and stir everything together.
5. At this point, you pour 1 can of Coors Light (or better still other low carb beer, or ½ Cup Red Wine) into the pan.
6. This is when you add mushrooms and spinach and mix everything in together.
7. Finally, once spinach has wilted, add ketchup, mix, and serve!

Creamy Spinach Pork Tenderloin Roulade

Nutritional value:

Note: this makes 4 servings in total.

Per serving

483 Calories

31.5g Fats

2.5g Net Carbs

36.5g Protein.

Ingredients:

3 tablespoons + 1 teaspoon of Olive Oil

5 slices of Prosciutto

4 oz. of Cream Cheese

Salt and Pepper (to taste)

1 lb. of Pork Tenderloin

2 teaspoons + 1 teaspoon of Minced Garlic

6-7 cups of Spinach

¼ teaspoon of Mrs. Dash Table Blend

Directions:

1. Meanwhile, you heat oven to 450F.
2. After which, you bitterly the pork tenderloin by cutting 1 or 2 strips through the meat of the pork.
3. After that, you put plastic wrap over pork and pound out the meat to ½ inch thickness using the smooth side of the meat hammer.
4. Then you season with salt and pepper and pound lightly with the spiked side of meat hammer.
5. At this point, you add olive oil to the pan can bring to high heat.

6. This is when you add garlic and let cook for about 30-60 seconds, then add spinach and sauté until wilted.
7. Furthermore, you lay slices of prosciutto over pork tenderloin to cover the entire surface.
8. Pour spinach over the pork tenderloin. (NOTE: make sure all the oil gets in there too.)
9. After that, you rip pieces of cream cheese off and lay them on the pork.
10. After which you roll the pork up and use toothpicks to secure the end. Feel free to use butchers string to do this.
11. Then you add seasonings to outside of pork (preferably, pepper, Mrs. Dash, and minced garlic).
12. Finally, you bake for about 20 minutes at 450F and then reduce heat to 325F and cook for 60-75 minutes until internal temperature reads 145F.

Keto Paprika Chicken

Nutritional value:

Note: this makes 4 total servings.

Per serving

274 Calories

13.6g Fats

2g Net Carbs

36.4g Protein.

Ingredients:

3 Tablespoons of Olive Oil

2 Tablespoons of Lemon Juice (1 Lemon)

Salt and Pepper

4 Boneless, Skinless Chicken Breasts

2 Tablespoons of Spanish Smoked Paprika

1 Tablespoons of Maple Syrup

2 teaspoons of Minced Garlic

Directions:

1. Meanwhile, you heat oven to 350F.
2. After which you prep chicken by cutting into chunks and seasoning with salt and pepper.
3. After that, you prep sauce by combining all other ingredients.
4. Then you add 1/3 of sauce to the bottom of a casserole dish and lay chicken on top of it.
5. At this point, you spread to rest of sauce thoroughly over all pieces of chicken, then put in the oven for 30-35 minutes.
6. Finally, to finish the chicken off, broil for an additional 4-5 minutes.

Low Carb Chicken Satay

Nutritional value:

Yields 3 servings.

Each serving

393 Calories

23g Fats

3.7g Net Carbs

35g Protein.

Ingredients:

4 Tablespoons of Soy Sauce

2 Spring of Onions

1 Tablespoon of Erythritol

2 teaspoons of Sesame Oil

1 teaspoon of Minced Garlic

Juice of ½ Lime

1 lb. of Ground Chicken

3 Tablespoons of Peanut Butter

1/3 Yellow Pepper

1 Tablespoon of Rice Vinegar

2 teaspoons of Chili Paste

¼ teaspoon of Cayenne

¼ teaspoon of Paprika

Directions:

1. First, you heat 2 teaspoons of sesame oil on medium-high heat in a pan.
2. After which you brown ground chicken, then add all other ingredients.

3. After that, you mix well and continue cooking.
4. Then once everything is cooked, add 2 chopped spring onions and 1/3 sliced yellow pepper.

Baked Sea Bass with Herb Cauliflower Salad

Nutritional value:

Note: this makes a total of 2 servings of Baked Sea Bass with Herbed Cauliflower Salad.

Each serving

380 Calories

25.98g Fats

3.39g Net Carbs

27.52g Protein.

Ingredients:

1/3 cup of fresh mint

3 tablespoons of extra virgin olive oil

1/3 cup of green olives

Salt and pepper (to taste)

1/3 cup of flat leaf parsley

10 ounces' whole sea bass (cleaned and scaled)

1 cup of finely grated cauliflower

2 small lemon

Directions:

1. Meanwhile, you heat the oven to 400°F.
2. After which you finely chop the parsley and mint.
3. After that, you prepare the sea bass by placing on baking parchment in a baking dish and rub with 1 tablespoon extra-virgin olive oil.
4. This you season with salt and pepper.
5. At this point, you thinly slice one of the lemons then stuff into the sea bass with a small amount of the fresh herbs.

6. After which you bake in the oven for 15 minutes, or until the thickest part of the fish is cooked.
7. In the meantime, finely chop the olives. Zest and juice the other lemon.
8. Furthermore, in a large bowl mix together the grated cauliflower, lemon zest, herbs, olives, lemon juice and 2 tablespoons of extra virgin olive oil.
9. After that, you season with salt and pepper to taste.
10. Finally, you remove the sea bass from the oven when cooked and serve with the herbed cauliflower salad.

Spicy Cauliflower Rice & Salmon Medley

Nutritional value:

Note: this makes a total of 6 servings of Spicy Cauliflower Rice & Salmon Medley.

Each serving

232.83 Calories

14.21g Fats

5.05g Net Carbs

17.38g Protein.

Ingredients:

4 (about 4-oz) fillets salmon (cubed into 2-inch pieces)

1 medium (about 119 g) orange bell pepper (chopped)

4 tablespoons of soy sauce

2 tablespoons of Japanese 7-spice (shichimi togarashi)

Salt and pepper (to taste)

2 tablespoons of olive oil

1 small (50 g) carrot (chopped)

2 tablespoons of (20 g) shallot (finely diced)

2 tablespoons of sesame oil

1 medium (588 g) cauliflower (diced)

Directions:

1. First, in a medium sized stock-pot, preheat your olive oil on medium heat.
2. After which you sauté the salmon cubes for about 5 minutes, stirring occasionally until they have gone from pink to white.
3. After that, you add in the carrot, peppers, and shallots.
4. Then you sauté for 5 minutes.

5. At this point, you stir in the soy sauce and sesame oil, making sure you coat all the vegetables and fish.
6. Furthermore, you season the veggies with the 7-spice powder then stir and let the fish soak up the soy and sesame for 2-3 minutes.
7. After that, you add the cauliflower rice and mix in with a wooden spoon.
8. Then you turn your stove up to medium-high to fry the cauliflower; stir occasionally.
9. Finally, you taste! Use a little more spice if needed, then season with salt and pepper.

Low Carb Sweet and Sour Meatballs

Nutritional value:

Note: this makes a total of 5 servings of Sweet and Sour Meatballs.

Each serving

295.4 Calories

18.66g Fats

5.35g Net Carbs

28.26g Protein.

Ingredients:

The meatballs:

1 large egg

½ teaspoon of onion powder

1 pound of ground beef

¼ cup of Parmesan cheese

Ingredients for the sauce:

¼ cup of apple cider vinegar

1/3 cup of sugar-free ketchup

½ teaspoon of xanthan gum

1 ½ cups of water

3 tablespoons of soy sauce

1 cup of erythritol

Directions:

1. First, in a large mixing bowl add ground beef, an egg, grated Parmesan cheese, and onion powder.
2. After which you mix together with your hands.
3. After that, you use a tablespoon to measure, shape the meatballs. (NOTE: You should be able to form 30 mini meatballs.)

4. Meanwhile, you heat a saucepan over medium heat.
5. Then you add the meatballs and cook until browned on the outside. (NOTE: If it's slightly pink in the middle, that's okay for now.); put to the side.
6. Furthermore, in the same sauce pan add the water, soy sauce, apple cider vinegar, sugar-free ketchup, and erythritol.
7. After which you use a whisk to stir until the sauce comes together.
8. After that, you slowly whisk in the xanthan gum. (NOTE: stir in a little at a time, waiting a couple minutes in between to make sure it thickens.)
9. At this point, you lower the temperature, and let the sauce simmer on low.
10. Then after a couple of minutes, check the sauce to make sure it's the desired consistency. (NOTE: feel free to dip a spoon into the sauce to see if it coats the back.)
11. Remember, if you run your finger across the back of the spoon, a thickened sauce will not immediately run back together. Careful not to burn yourself.
12. Finally, you add the meatballs and let them simmer on low for 10 minutes or until the meatballs are fully cooked through.

Hassel back Marinara Chicken

Nutritional value:

Note: this makes a total of 6 servings of Hassel back Marinara Chicken.

Each serving

338 Calories

18.28g Fats

2.56g Net Carbs

37.96g Protein.

Ingredients:

1/3 cup of shredded mozzarella

3 whole chicken breasts

2/3 cup of Rao's homemade (tomato basil sauce)

salt and pepper (to taste)

4 ounces of cream cheese

10 ounce of package frozen spinach (thawed with water squeezed out)

1 tablespoon of olive oil

3 ounces of mozzarella slices

Directions:

1. Meanwhile, you heat your oven to 400°F.
2. After which you place the cream cheese, mozzarella, and spinach in a microwave safe bowl.
3. After that, you heat for about 2 minutes, or until the cheeses get melty and can be easily mixed together.
4. Then you mix the filling and add salt and pepper to taste.
5. At this point, you cut several horizontal slices across each chicken breast, cut as deeply as you can without slicing all the way through the chicken.
6. After that, you season the chicken with salt and pepper.

7. This is when you stuff each piece of chicken with the cheese filling.
8. Furthermore, you brush some olive oil onto the bare chicken tops.
9. After which, you cook for 25 minutes, or until chicken reaches 165°F.
10. At this point, you change your oven to the broil setting.
11. Then you top with Rao's tomato sauce, and the slices of mozzarella.
12. Finally, you broil for 5 minutes, or until the cheese gets melty and starts to brown.

Low Carb Sweet and Sour Meatballs

Nutritional value:

Note: this makes a total of 5 servings of Sweet and Sour Meatballs.

Each serving

295.4 Calories

18.66g Fats

5.35g Net Carbs

28.26g Protein.

Ingredients:

The meatballs:

1 large egg

½ teaspoon of onion powder

1 pound of ground beef

¼ cup of Parmesan cheese

Ingredients for the sauce:

¼ cup of apple cider vinegar

1/3 cup of sugar-free ketchup

½ teaspoon of xanthan gum

1 ½ cups of water

3 tablespoons of soy sauce

1 cup of erythritol

Directions:

1. First, in a large mixing bowl add ground beef, an egg, grated Parmesan cheese, and onion powder.
2. After which you mix together with your hands.

3. After that, you use a tablespoon to measure, shape the meatballs. (NOTE: You should be able to form 30 mini meatballs.)
4. Meanwhile, you heat a saucepan over medium heat.
5. Then you add the meatballs and cook until browned on the outside. (NOTE: If it's slightly pink in the middle, that's okay for now.); Put to the side.
6. Furthermore, in the same sauce pan add the water, sugar-free ketchup, apple cider vinegar, soy sauce, and erythritol.
7. After that, you use a whisk to stir until the sauce comes together.
8. Furthermore, you slowly whisk in the xanthan gum. (NOTE: stir in a little at a time, waiting a couple minutes in between to make sure it thickens.)
9. After which you lower the temperature, and let the sauce simmer on low.
10. Then after a couple of minutes, check the sauce to make sure it's the desired consistency. Dip a spoon into the sauce to see if it coats the back.
11. Remember, if you run your finger across the back of the spoon, a thickened sauce will not immediately run back together. Careful not to burn yourself.
12. Finally, you add the meatballs, and let them simmer on low for about 10 minutes or until the meatballs are fully cooked through.

Savory Italian Egg Bake

Ingredients:

3 tablespoons of mustard

½ cup of heavy whipping cream

2 cups of diced cooked chicken breast

½ cup of grated Parmesan cheese

1 cup of shredded extra sharp cheese

10 large eggs

2 teaspoons of garlic and herb seasoning

½ cup of tomato sauce

12 ounces of frozen broccoli florets

1 teaspoon of parsley flakes

Directions:

1. Meanwhile, you heat oven to 350°F.
2. After that, in a large mixing bowl, whisk together the eggs.
3. Then whisk in the mustard, garlic and herb seasoning, and heavy whipping cream.
4. At this point, when that's blended well, slowly whisk in the tomato sauce until it's no longer lumpy.
5. This is when you add in the diced chicken and broccoli florets.
6. Furthermore, you crease a casserole dish or a large baking pan then pour in the Italian bake.
7. After which, you sprinkle Parmesan cheese and parsley flakes on top of the Italian bake.
8. After that, you bake for 30-40 minutes at 350°F, or until the top looks like a crust.
9. Then before serving, I suggest you top the Italian bake with some sharp extra sharp cheese. (**NOTE:** feel free to use any other cheese that you like, such as mozzarella or pepper jack.)

Skillet Browned Chicken with Creamy Greens

Ingredients:

2 Tablespoons of coconut oil

1 cup of cream

2 cups of dark leafy greens

Salt and pepper (to taste)

1 lb. of chicken thighs (boneless but skin on)

1 cup of chicken stock

1 teaspoon of Italian herbs

2 Tablespoons of butter (melted)

2 Tablespoons of coconut flour

Directions:

1. Meanwhile, you heat a large skillet on a medium-high setting.
2. After which you add two tablespoons of coconut oil to the pan.
3. After that, you season both sides of the chicken thighs with salt and pepper while the oil heats up.
4. Then you brown chicken thighs in the skillet.
5. At this point, you fry both sides until the chicken is cooked through and crispy.
6. Then, while the thighs are cooking you should start the sauce.
7. If you want to create the sauce, first, you melt two tablespoons of butter in a sauce pan.
8. Furthermore, once the butter stops sizzling, whisk in two tablespoons of coconut flour to form a thick paste.
9. After which you whisk in one cup of cream and bring the mixture to a boil. (NOTE: The mixture should thicken after a few minutes.
10. After that, you stir in the teaspoon of Italian herbs.
11. This is when you remove cooked chicken thighs from the skillet and set aside.
12. Then you pour the cup of chicken stock into the chicken skillet and deglaze the pan.
13. Whisk in the cream sauce and stir the greens into the pan so that they become coated with the sauce.

14. Finally, you lay the chicken thighs back on top of the greens, then remove from the heat and serve.
15. Divide chicken and greens up into four servings size.

Spicy Sausage & Cabbage Skillet Melt

Ingredients:

1 ½ cups of green cabbage (shredded)

½ cup of diced onion

2 Tablespoons of chopped fresh cilantro

4 spicy Italian chicken sausages

1 ½ cups of purple cabbage (shredded)

2 Tablespoons of coconut oil

2 slices (about 1 ounce each) of Colby Jack cheese

Directions:

1. First, you remove casings from sausages and rough chop.
2. After which you chop the onion and shred cabbage (if you not using pre-shredded cabbage.)
3. After that, you melt coconut oil in a large skillet and add onion and cabbage.
4. Then you cook over medium-high heat until the vegetables begin to become tender, about 8 minutes.
5. This is when you add sausage, stirring to mix it into the cabbage and onions.
6. Furthermore, you cook 8 minutes more.
7. After which you add the cheese on top and cover the skillet.
8. Then you turn off the heat and wait 5 minutes while the cheese melts into the cabbage and vegetables.
9. After that, you remove the lid from the skillet and stir.
10. Finally, you top with cilantro and serve immediately right from the skillet.

Reverse Seared Ribeye Steak

Nutritional value:

Note: this makes a total of 3 servings of Reverse Seared Ribeye Steak.

Each ~6.5 oz. serving

430 Calories

31.7g Fats

0g Net Carbs

30.3g Protein.

Ingredients:

3 tablespoons of Bacon Fat (or better still other high smoke point oil)

2 medium Ribeye Steaks (about 1.2 lbs.)

Salt and Pepper (to Taste)

Directions:

1. Meanwhile, heat oven to 250F.
2. After which you put your steaks on a wire rack on top of a cookie sheet.
3. After that, season heavily with salt and pepper on all sides.
4. Then you stick an instant-read thermometer through the side of the steak.
5. At this point, you bake in the oven until internal temperature of 123F is reached.
6. After that, you heat the bacon grease in a cast iron skillet and wait until the pan is very hot.
7. Finally, you place the steaks in and sear for 30 - 45 seconds on each side.

Keto Tater Tot Nachos (AKA Totchos)

Nutritional value:

Note: this makes 2 total servings of Keto Tater Tot Nachos (AKA Totchos).

Each serving

637 Calories

52.5g Fats

5.5g Net Carbs

32.3g Protein.

Ingredients:

6 oz. of Ground Beef (80/20), cooked

2 tablespoons of Sour Cream

½ medium Jalapeno Pepper (sliced)

2 servings of Keto Tater Tots

2 oz. of Cheddar Cheese (shredded)

6 Black Olives (sliced)

1 tablespoon of Salsa

Directions:

1. First, in a small casserole dish or mini cast iron skillet, lay down 9-10 Keto tater tots.
2. After which you add ½ ground beef, and ½ of the shredded cheese.
3. After that, you start the second layer with fewer tater tots, ½ of the remaining beef, and ½ of the remaining cheese. (NOTE: repeat with the last of the tater tots.)
4. This is when you broil in the oven for 4-5 minutes so that the cheese melts.
5. Then you serve with jalapenos, sour cream, black olives, and salsa.
6. Enjoy!

Blackberry Chipotle Chicken Wings

Nutritional value:

Note: this makes a total of 20 Blackberry Chipotle Chicken Wings.

Per 4 wings

503 Calories

39.1g Fats

1.8g Net Carbs

34.5g Protein.

Ingredients:

½ cup of Blackberry Chipotle Jam

Salt and Pepper (to Taste)

3 lbs. of Chicken Wings (about 20 wings, butchered)

½ cup of Water

Directions:

1. First, you butcher the chicken wings by separating drum mettes, wings, and wing tips.
2. After which you freeze wing tips for use in bone broth.
3. After that, you combine Blackberry Chipotle Jam and water in a bowl.
4. This is when you whisk to combine, then add 2/3 marinade with the chicken wings in a plastic bag.
5. At this point, you season with salt and pepper to taste.
6. Furthermore, you let this sit for at least 30 minutes, or overnight.
7. Then, once ready, preheat oven to 400F.
8. This is when you lay chicken on a cookie sheet with a wire rack on top.
9. After that, you bake for 15 minutes at 400F, then flip and turn the oven up to 425F.
10. Finally, you brush the remaining marinade over each wing (now the bottom side) and bake for 20-30 minutes.

Keto Chicken Pad Thai

Nutritional value:

Note: this makes a total of 4 servings of Keto Chicken Pad Thai.

Each serving

431 Calories

35.3g Fats

5g Net Carbs

26.3g Protein.

Ingredients:

Pad Thai Sauce

Juice of 1/3 Lemon

½ teaspoon of Worcestershire Sauce

1 ½ tablespoon of Sambal Olek

1 tablespoon of Natural Peanut Butter

7 drops of Liquid Stevia

Juice of ½ Lime

1 ½ tablespoons of Reduced Sugar Ketchup

3 tablespoons of Red Boat Fish Sauce

1 ½ teaspoons of Minced Garlic

1 teaspoon of Rice Wine Vinegar

Noodles and Toppings

3 medium Green Onions (chopped)

2 packets of Shirataki Noodles

4 tablespoons of Coconut oil

2 tablespoons of Peanuts (chopped)

¼ cup of Cilantro (chopped)

2 large Eggs

3 medium Chicken Thighs

4 oz. of Mung Bean Sprouts

Directions:

1. First, you mix together all of the ingredients for the sauce using a fork or whisk; Set aside.
2. After which you drain shirataki noodles and rinse well (NOTE: repeat 5 or 6 times, then dry as much as you can use a cloth, wringing out as needed.)
3. After that, you debone and desk in chicken thighs then cut into cubed pieces.
4. At this point, you heat 2 tablespoons of Coconut Oil in a pan over medium-high heat.
5. Then, once the pan is hot, add the chicken to create a sear.
6. Furthermore, you flip chicken pieces over to sear the other side.
7. This is when you set aside and repeat with the rest of the chicken (using more oil).
8. Then, in the same pan, you add the shirataki noodles and dry fry them for 5-8 minutes or until noodles become firmer to the touch.
9. After which you reduce heat and scramble 2 eggs into the noodles.
10. After that, you add the sauce, chicken (including oil), cilantro, and green onion to the noodles.
11. Finally, you let this cook down for about 5-10 minutes depending on the thickness you want.

Hearty Crock Pot Chicken Stew

Nutritional value:

Note: this makes about 5 big servings,

365 Calories

20g Fat

7.6g Carbs

Ingredients:

1 Medium Green Pepper

1 ½ Cup of Tomato Sauce (I prefer Classico Tomato and Basil)

1/3 Cup of Hot Wing Sauce

2 teaspoons of Ranch Seasoning

2 teaspoons of Paprika

1 teaspoon of Oregano

3 lbs. of Chicken Thigh

3 Cups of Mushrooms

½ Cup of Sliced Tomatoes

3 Tablespoons of Butter

2 teaspoons of Minced Garlic

1 teaspoon of Red Pepper Flakes

Directions:

1. First, you chop mushrooms and pepper into thin slices.
2. After which you turn crock pot to high heat.
3. After that, you add chicken thighs, garlic, tomato sauce, slide tomato, spices, and hot sauce to crock pot.
4. Then you add peppers and onions to chicken mixture, mix thoroughly.
5. This is when you let simmer on high for 2 hours.
6. At this point, you turn crock pot to low, stir ingredients.
7. After that, you allow cooking for another 3-5 hours.

8. Then you add 3 tablespoons of butter to your stew and stir together. (Optional: ½ teaspoon of xanthan gum for thickening.)
9. Finally, you cook for another hour without the lid so the sauce can reduce.
10. You can serve hot and enjoy or better still store it in the fridge and reheat for meals later in the microwave.

40 Minute Fresh Keto Chili

Nutritional value:

Note: this makes about 6 servings,

each serving being:

404.33 Calories

27.06g Fat

5.11g Carbs

31.09g Protein.

Ingredients:

8 cups of Spinach (about 8 oz.)

¼ cup of Parmesan Cheese

2/3 medium Onion

1 Tablespoon of Cumin

2 teaspoons of Cayenne Pepper

Salt and Pepper (to Taste)

2 lbs. of Ground Beef (85/15)

1 cup of Rao's Tomato Sauce

2 mediums Green Bell Peppers

1 Tablespoon of Olive Oil

1 ½ Tablespoons of Chili Powder

1 teaspoon of Garlic Powder

Directions:

1. First, you chop the onion and bell peppers to the size of your liking.
2. After which you season with salt/pepper and sauté in olive oil on medium-high heat stirring occasionally.

3. Then, once the beef is browned, reduce the heat of the vegetables to low and let cook.
4. After that, you put your ground beef in a pot over medium-high heat and start to brown it.
5. This is when you season with salt, pepper, and spices.
6. Furthermore, once the beef is browned, add the spinach to the pot.
7. After that, let stream for 2-3 minutes, then mix in well.
8. Then you add low carb tomato sauce to the pot, stir well, then reduce heat to medium-low and cook for 10 minutes.
9. Finally, you add the parmesan cheese and then stir together, then add the vegetables in and stir again.
10. At this point, you let cook for a few more minutes and serve with toppings of your choice when ready.

Delectable Keto Snacks Recipes

Cheesy Cauliflower Onion Dip

Ingredients:

1 ½ cups of chicken broth

¼ cup of mayonnaise

½ teaspoon of ground cumin

½ teaspoon of garlic powder

½ teaspoon of salt

1 pound or 1 large head cauliflower

½ cup of medium-sized onion

¾ cup of cream cheese

½ teaspoon of chili powder

½ teaspoon of ground black pepper

Directions:

1. First, you simmer the cauliflower and half an onion in chicken broth until soft and tender.
2. After which you stir in the cumin, garlic powder, chili powder, pepper, and salt.
3. After that, you cut up chunks of cream cheese, and whisk into the cauliflower until the cream cheese melts and is no longer chunky.
4. Then you use a stick blender, or a regular blender, to blend the mixture until it's smooth.
5. At this point, you carefully whisk in the mayonnaise.
6. Finally, you chill in the fridge 2-3 hours before serving.

Pesto Keto Crackers

Ingredients:

¼ teaspoon of ground black pepper

½ teaspoon of baking powder

Pinch of cayenne pepper

3 Tablespoons of butter

1 ¼ cups of almond flour

½ teaspoon of salt

¼ teaspoon of dried basil

1 clove of garlic (pressed)

2 Tablespoons of basil pesto

Directions:

1. Meanwhile, you heat oven to 325 degrees Fahrenheit.
2. After which you line a cookie sheet with parchment paper.
3. Then, in a medium bowl, combine almond flour, pepper, salt and baking powder and whisk until smooth.
4. After that, you add basil, cayenne, and garlic and stir until evenly combined.
5. Then add in the pesto and whisk until the dough forms into coarse crumbs.
6. At this point, you cut the butter into the cracker mixture with a fork or your fingers until the dough forms into a ball.
7. This is when you transfer the dough onto the prepared cookie sheet and spread out the dough thinly until it's about 1 ½ mm thick. (NOTE: Make sure the thickness is the same throughout so that the crackers bake evenly.)
8. Furthermore, you place the pan in the preheated oven and bake for 14-17 minutes until light golden brown in color.
9. Once the dough has finished baking, I suggest is time to remove it from the oven.
10. Finally, you cut into crackers of the desired size or break into pieces.

Neapolitan Fat Bombs

Nutritional value:

Note: this makes a total of 24 Neapolitan Fat Bombs.

Each fat bomb

102 Calories

10.9g Fats

0.4g Net Carbs

0.6g Protein.

Ingredients:

½ of cup Coconut Oil

½ cup of Cream Cheese

2 tablespoons of Erythritol

1 teaspoon of Vanilla Extract

½ cup of Butter

½ cup of Sour Cream

2 tablespoons of Cocoa Powder

25 drops of Liquid Stevia

2 medium Strawberries

Directions:

1. First, you combine all ingredients (except for cocoa powder, vanilla, and strawberries) in a bowl.
2. After which you use an immersion blender to mix it together.
3. After that, you separate the mixture between 3 bowls.
4. Then you add cocoa powder to one, vanilla to another, and strawberries to the last.
5. At this point, you pour chocolate mixture into fat bomb mold, then freeze for 30 minutes. (NOTE: repeat with vanilla and strawberry layers.)
6. Finally, you let freeze for at least 1 hour.

Coconut Orange Creamsicle Fat Bombs

Nutritional value:

Note: this makes a total of 10 Coconut Orange Creamsicle Fat Bombs.

Each fat bomb

176 Calories,

20g Fats

0.7g Net Carbs

0.8g Protein.

Ingredients:

½ cup of Heavy Whipping Cream

10 drops of Liquid Stevia

½ cup of coconut oil

4 oz. of Cream Cheese

1 tsp. of Orange Vanilla Mio

Directions:

1. First, you use an immersion blender to blend together all of the ingredients. (NOTE: If you're having a hard time blending the ingredients, you can microwave them to soften them up.)
2. After which you spread the mixture into a silicone tray and freeze for 2-3 hours.
3. Then, once hardened, remove from the silicone tray and store in the freezer.

Savory Pizza Fat Bombs

Nutritional value:

Note: this makes a total of 6 Pizza Fat Bombs.

Each fat bomb

110 Calories

10.5g Fats

1.3g Net Carbs

2.3g Protein.

Ingredients:

14 slices Pepperoni

2 tablespoons of Sun Dried Tomato Pesto

Salt and Pepper (to Taste)

4 oz. of Cream Cheese

8 pitted Black Olives

2 tablespoons of Fresh Basil (chopped)

Directions:

1. First, you dice pepperoni and olives into small pieces.
2. After which you mix together all of the ingredients.
3. Then, you form into balls, then garnish with pepperoni, basil, and olive.

No Bake Chocolate Peanut Butter Fat Bombs

Nutritional value:

Note: this makes a total of 8 No Bake Chocolate Peanut Butter Fat Bombs.

Each fat bomb

208 Calories

20g Fats

0.8g Net Carbs

4.4g Protein.

Ingredients:

¼ cup of cocoa powder

6 tablespoons of Shelled Hemp Seeds

1 teaspoon of Vanilla Extract

¼ cup of Unsweetened Shredded Coconut

½ cup of Coconut Oil

4 tablespoons of PB Fit Powder

2 tablespoons of Heavy Cream

28 drops of Liquid Stevia

Directions:

1. First, you mix together all of the dry ingredients with the coconut oil. (NOTE: it may take a bit of work, but it will eventually turn into a paste.)
2. After which you add heavy cream, vanilla, and liquid stevia.
3. After that, you mix again until everything is combined and slightly creamy.
4. Then you measure out unsweetened shredded coconut on to a plate.
5. At this point, you roll balls out using your hand and then roll in the unsweetened shredded coconut.
6. Finally, you lay on to a baking tray covered with parchment paper.
7. Then you set in the freezer for about 20 minutes.

Smoked Salmon and Goat Cheese Bites

Nutritional value:

Note: this makes a total of 16 servings of Smoked Salmon & Goat Cheese Bites.

Each serving

46.19 Calories

3.33g Fats

0.94g Net Carbs

3.43g Protein.

Ingredients:

1 tablespoon (about 2 g) fresh oregano

1 tablespoon (about 2.65 g) fresh basil

Salt and pepper (to taste)

4 ounces (about 113.4 g) smoked salmon

8 ounces (about 228 g) goat cheese (softened)

1 tablespoon (about 1.7 g) fresh rosemary

2 cloves (about 6 g) garlic

3.9 ounces (about 110 g) radicchio

Directions:

1. First, you finely mince the oregano, rosemary, and fresh basil.
2. After which you finely grate the garlic.
3. After that, you add the goat cheese, salt, herbs, garlic, and pepper to a mixing bowl.
4. This is when you combine well then set aside.
5. Furthermore, you cut the stem off the bottom of the radicchio. (NOTE: Carefully peel apart the leaves until you have 16 leaves for serving.) I prefer to use more of the inner leaves for their size and shape. Feel free to save any leftover radicchio for other salads or recipes. Wash and dry the leaves then.

6. Then, on each radicchio leave lay a piece of smoked salmon than a ½ ounce of the herbed goat cheese.
7. Finally, you sprinkle some black pepper on the top then serve.

Feta and Bacon Bites

Nutritional value:

Note: this makes a total of 24 servings of Feta and Bacon Bites.

Each serving

71.79 Calories

5.74g Fats

1.08g Net Carbs

3.66g Protein.

Ingredients:

2 cups of shredded mozzarella

¼ cup of crumbled feta cheese

Salt and pepper (to taste)

¾ cup of almond flour

8 slices bacon (cooked)

¼ cup chopped green onions

3 tablespoons of sriracha mayo (like Sarayo)

Directions:

1. Meanwhile, you heat your oven to 350°F
2. After which in a nonstick pan over medium heat, combine your almond flour and mozzarella; stir constantly.
3. Remember that the flour/cheese mix will form a dough like consistency after about 5 minutes.
4. After that, you place your dough between two pieces of parchment paper.
5. Then you roll flat with a rolling pin.
6. At this point, you use a cookie cutter or glass to cut out 24 circles. (NOTE: if you run out of dough then form the remaining bits into a ball.)

7. After that, you heat it up on the stove, then roll it out again.
8. This is when you place the circles of dough into your muffin tin (or on a cookie sheet.)
9. After which you top with the bacon, feta, and onions.
10. Then you bake at 350°F for about 15 minutes, until the edges are browned.
11. Finally, you cool, peel off the liners, and top with sriracha mayo!

Feta and Bacon Bites

Nutritional value:

Note: this makes a total of 24 servings of Feta and Bacon Bites.

Each serving

71.79 Calories

5.74g Fats

1.08g Net Carbs

3.66g Protein.

Ingredients:

2 cups of shredded mozzarella

¼ cup of crumbled feta cheese

3 tablespoons of sriracha mayo (like Sarayo)

Salt and pepper (to taste)

¾ cup of almond flour

8 slices bacon (cooked)

¼ cup chopped green onions

Directions:

1. Meanwhile, you heat your oven to 350°F
2. After which, in a nonstick pan over medium heat, combine your almond flour and mozzarella; stir constantly.
3. Remember, the flour/cheese mix will form a dough like consistency after about 5 minutes.
4. After that, you place your dough between two pieces of parchment paper.
5. Then you roll flat with a rolling pin.
6. Furthermore, you use a cookie cutter or glass to cut out 24 circles. (NOTE: If you run out of dough, I suggest you form the remaining bits into a ball.)

7. After that, you heat it up on the stove, then roll it out again.
8. After which you place the circles of dough into your muffin tin (or on a cookie sheet.)
9. Then you top with the bacon, feta, and onions.
10. This is when you bake at 350°F for about 15 minutes until the edges are browned.
11. Finally, you cool, peel off the liners, and top with sriracha mayo!

Spicy Sausage Cheese Dip

Ingredients:

1 (about 15-ounce) can of Rotel Hot Diced Tomato (with Habaneros)

8 ounces of cream cheese

8 ounces of diced pepper jack cheese

1 pound of hot Italian ground sausage

¼ cup of sliced green onions

16 ounces of sour cream

Directions:

1. First, you use a saucepan, cook the hot Italian sausage on medium until lightly browned.
2. After which you stir in the can of Rotel and cook for a few minutes.
3. After that, you mix in the green onions and turn off the heat when the Italian sausage has fully browned.
4. Then you set a slow cooker on high then layer the bottom of the stoneware with the pepper jack cheese, and cream cheese cut into chunks.
5. At this point, you pour the Italian sausage on top of the cheese.
6. This is when you spread the sour cream on top of the Italian sausage.
7. Furthermore, after about an hour, stir the dip until the cheese is completely incorporated.
8. Allow to continue cooking, then after about two hours on high until the dip is completely done.

Jalapeno Popper Fat Bombs

Nutritional value:

Note: this makes a total of 3 Jalapeno Popper Fat Bombs.

Each fat bomb

207 Calories

19.3g Fats

1.5g Net Carb

4.8g Protein.

Ingredients:

3 slices of Bacon

½ teaspoon of Dried Parsley

Salt and Pepper (to Taste)

3 oz. of Cream Cheese

1 medium Jalapeno Pepper

¼ teaspoon of Onion Powder

¼ teaspoon of Garlic Powder

Directions:

1. First, you fry 3 slices of bacon until crisp, set aside on paper towels; save bacon grease.
2. After which, you de-seed a jalapeno pepper, then dice into small pieces.
3. After that, you mix together with cream cheese, bacon fat, and spices; season to taste.
4. At this point, you crumble bacon and set on a plate.
5. Finally, you roll cream cheese mixture into balls using your hand, then roll the ball into the bacon.

Keto Corndog Muffins

Nutritional value:

Note: this makes 20 Keto Corndog Muffins.

Each muffin

79 Calories

6.8g Fats

0.7g Net Carbs

2.4g Protein.

Ingredients:

½ cup of Flaxseed Meal

3 tablespoons of Swerve Sweetener

¼ teaspoon of Baking Powder

1 large Egg

10 Lit'l Smokies (or preferably 3 hot dogs)

½ cup of Blanched Almond Flour

1 tablespoon of Psyllium Husk Powder

¼ teaspoon of Salt

¼ cup of Butter (melted)

1/3 cup of Sour Cream

¼ cup of Coconut Milk

Directions:

1. Meanwhile, you heat oven to 375F.
2. After which you mix together all of the dry ingredients in a bowl.
3. After that, you add egg, sour cream, coconut milk, and butter and then mix well.
4. Then you divide the batter up between 20 well-greased mini-muffin slots.

5. At this point, you slice Lit'l Smokies in half and insert into the middle of each muffin.
6. Furthermore, you bake for 12 minutes and then broil for 1-2 minutes until the tops are lightly browned. (NOTE: If needed, push the pieces of the hot dog back into the muffin if they rose with the batter.)
7. Finally, you let the muffins cool for a few minutes in the tray, then remove and let cool on a wire rack.

NOTE: always remember that you can also mix together mayonnaise, ketchup, and chili paste to make a sweet and spicy dipping sauce!

Keto Tropical Smoothie

Nutritional value:

Nate: this makes 1 Keto Tropical Smoothie.

For the whole thing,

352 Calories

31g Fats

3g Net Carbs

5g Protein.

Ingredients:

2 tablespoons of Golden Flaxseed Meal

¼ cup of Sour Cream

1 tablespoon of MCT Oil

¼ teaspoon of Banana Extract

7 Ice Cubes

3/4 cup of Unsweetened Coconut Milk

20 drops of Liquid Stevia

½ teaspoon of Mango Extract

¼ teaspoon of Blueberry Extract

Directions:

1. First, you add all ingredients together into a blender. (NOTE: I suggest you wait a few minutes so that the flax meal has enough time to soak up some of the moisture.)
2. Then you blend for 1-2 minutes until everything is incorporated well, then serve up!

Cucumber Spinach Smoothie

Ingredients:

2.5 oz. of Cucumber (peeled and cubed)

1 cup of Coconut Milk (from carton)

1-2 tablespoons of MCT Oil

2 handfuls of Spinach

7 ice Cubes

12 drops of Liquid Stevia

¼ teaspoon of Xanthan Gum

Directions:

1. First, you add all ingredients to a blender.
2. After which you blend everything together for 1-2 minutes or until the consistency is good for you.
3. Then you pour out and enjoy!

Layered Fried Queso Blanco

Ingredients:

1 ½ tablespoons of Olive Oil

Pinch Red Pepper Flakes

5 oz. of Queso Blanco

2 oz. of Olives

Directions:

1. First, you chop cheese into cubes and place in the freezer.
2. After which you heat oil in a skillet until hot over medium-high heat.
3. After that, you add cheese cubes and brown as much as possible on all sides.
4. Then, you bring the cheese together and press down with a spatula.
5. This is when you cook cheese on each side, flipping half of the cheese into itself and flipping the cheese as you see fit.
6. Furthermore, you continue cooking the cheese, flipping and folding the cheese into itself, building layers of crisped cheese one after the other.
7. After that, you use a knife or another spatula, form a block of the cheese you have and seal off each side.
8. Finally, you remove from pan, let cool slightly, and cut into small cubes.
9. Serve!

Maple Pecan Fat Bomb Bars

Nutritional value:

Note: this makes 12 total servings of Maple Pecan Fat Bomb Bars.

Each serving

303 Calories

30.5g Fats

2g Net Carbs

4.9g Protein.

Ingredients:

2 cups of Pecan Halves

1 cup of Almond Flour

½ cup of Golden Flaxseed Meal

½ cup of Unsweetened Shredded Coconut

½ cup of Coconut Oil

¼ cup of Maple Syrup

¼ teaspoon of Liquid Stevia (about 25 drops)

Directions:

1. First, you toast pecans in the oven for about 6-8 minutes at 350F.
2. After which you remove from the oven and crush them in a plastic bag using a rolling pin.
3. After that, you add all dry ingredients to a bowl (including pecans) and mix together.
4. Then you add wet ingredients and mix into a crumbly dough.
5. At this point, you press into a casserole dish (11x7) and bake for 20-25 minutes at 350F.
6. Finally, you remove and cool completely, then refrigerate for at least 1 hour.
7. Then cut into slices and serve.

Delectable Keto Lunch Recipes

Savory Italian Egg Bake

Ingredients:

3 tablespoons of mustard

½ cup of heavy whipping cream

2 cups of diced cooked chicken breast

½ cup of grated Parmesan cheese

1 cup of shredded extra sharp cheese

10 large eggs

2 teaspoons of garlic and herb seasoning

½ cup of tomato sauce

12 ounces of frozen broccoli florets

1 teaspoon of parsley flakes

Directions:

1. Meanwhile, you heat oven to 350°F. In a large mixing bowl, whisk together the eggs.
2. After which you whisk in the mustard, garlic and herb seasoning, and heavy whipping cream.
3. Then, when that's blended well, slowly whisk in the tomato sauce until it's no longer lumpy.
4. After that, you add in the diced chicken and broccoli florets.
5. At this point, you grease a casserole dish or a large baking pan then pour in the Italian bake.
6. This is when you sprinkle Parmesan cheese and parsley flakes on top of the Italian bake.
7. Then you bake for about 30-40 minutes at 350°F, or until the top looks like a crust.

8. Remember, before serving, I want you to top the Italian bake with some sharp extra sharp cheese. NOTE: You could also use any other cheese of your choosing, such as mozzarella or pepper jack.

Sausage and Kale Soup

Ingredients:

1 Tablespoon of butter

1 medium carrot (peeled and diced)

2 tablespoons of red wine vinegar

1 teaspoon of dried basil

¼ to ½ teaspoon of crushed red pepper flakes

1 cup of heavy cream

3 cups of kale (chopped)

½ teaspoon of freshly ground black pepper

1 lb. of ground sweet Italian sausage

1 medium yellow onion (chopped)

2 cloves garlic (crushed)

1 teaspoon of dried oregano

1 teaspoon of dried rubbed sage

4 cups of low-sodium chicken broth

½ medium head cauliflower (cut into small florets)

½ to 1 teaspoon of sea salt (or to taste)

Directions:

1. First, you heat a large saucepan or Dutch oven over medium high heat.
2. After which you add ground sausage, breaking up the meat.
3. After that, you cook, stirring occasionally until browned and cooked through about 5 minutes.
4. Then you use a slotted spoon, to remove cooked sausage and allow to drain on a plate covered with paper towels.
5. Furthermore, you discard drippings, but do not wash pan.
6. After which you melt butter over medium heat.
7. Then, when bubbling subsides, add onion and carrot.

8. After that, you cook until onion begins to brown on the edges and becomes somewhat translucent.
9. This is when you stir garlic into onion and carrot mixture.
10. Cook one minute and add red wine vinegar and cook until syrupy, scraping up browned bits-about 1 minute.
11. At this point, you stir in oregano, basil, sage and red pepper flakes.
12. After that, you pour in the stock and heavy cream. Increase heat to medium high.
13. Then, when soup reaches a simmer, add cauliflower and turn heat down to medium-low.
14. Then you simmer uncovered until cauliflower is fork-tender, about 10 minutes.
15. Stir in kale and cooked sausage; cook 1 to 2 minutes longer, or until kale wilts and the sausage is reheated.
16. Finally, you season to taste with salt and pepper. (NOTE: the amount of salt needed may vary due to variation in brands of broth.)

Broccoli Chicken Zucchini Boats

Nutritional value:

Note: this makes a total of 2 servings of Broccoli Chicken Zucchini Boats.

Each serving

34g Fats

5g Net Carbs

30g Protein.

Ingredients:

2 tablespoons of Butter

1 cup of Broccoli

2 tablespoons of Sour Cream

Salt and Pepper (to taste)

10 oz. Zucchini (2 large zucchinis, hollowed out)

3 oz. Cheddar Cheese (shredded)

6 oz. Rotisserie Chicken (shredded)

1 stalk of Green Onion

Directions:

1. Meanwhile, you heat the oven to 400F and cut the zucchini you're using in half lengthwise.
2. After which you use a spoon, scoop out most of the zucchini until you're left with a shell about ½ - 1 cm thick.
3. After that, you pour 1 tablespoon of melted butter into each zucchini boat, season with salt/pepper and place them in the oven for about 20 minutes.
4. Then, while zucchini is cooking, shred your rotisserie chicken and measure out 6 oz.
5. At this point, you cut up broccoli florets into small pieces, and combine both with sour cream.
6. This is when you season with salt and pepper.

7. Then, once the zucchini is done, take them out and add your chicken and broccoli filling.
8. Furthermore, you sprinkle cheddar cheese and bake for an additional 10-15 minutes or until the cheese is melted and browning.
9. Finally, you garnish with chopped green onion and enjoy with more sour cream or mayo!

Keto Mug Lasagna

Nutritional value:

Note: this makes a total of 1servings of Keto Mug Lasagna.

Each serving

318 Calories

23.54g Fats

5.39g Net Carbs

20.45g Protein.

Ingredients:

3 tablespoons of Rao's marinara

3 ounces of whole milk mozzarella

1/3 (about 65 g) zucchini

2 tablespoons of whole milk ricotta

Directions:

1. First, you slice the zucchini into paper thin rounds. (NOTE: feel free to use a really sharp knife or a mandolin.)
2. After which, in the bottom of your dish add a tablespoon of the marinara.
3. After that, you layer on some of the zucchini.
4. Then you carefully spread out 1 tablespoon of ricotta.
5. This is when you add another tablespoon of marinara.
6. At this point, you layer on the second layer of zucchini, another tablespoon of ricotta, any leftover zucchini, and then the last tablespoon of marinara.
7. After that, you top with the mozzarella.
8. Finally, you microwave for about 3-4 minutes, depending on the strength of your microwave.
9. Remember that you can always sprinkle on a little oregano or Parmesan cheese if you like.

Salmon Patties with Fresh Herbs

Nutritional value:

Note: this makes a total of 5 servings of Salmon Patties with Fresh Herbs.

Each two patty serving:

418 Calories

25g Fats

2.63g Net Carbs

46g Protein.

Ingredients:

2 tablespoons of chopped fresh chives

¼ cup of grated Parmesan cheese

2 large eggs

Salt and pepper (to taste)

2 tablespoons of olive oil

2 (about 14.75-oz) cans pink salmon

¼ cup of chopped fresh dill

4 ounces' pork rinds (crushed)

1 teaspoon of lemon zest

½ cup of almond flour

Directions:

1. First, you open and drain both cans of pink salmon and then add to a large mixing bowl.
2. After which you mix the Parmesan cheese, crushed pork rinds, chives, dill, 2 large eggs, lemon zest, and the salt and pepper into the salmon.
3. After that, you form the salmon into 3 ounce balls. (NOTE: I usually end up with about 10.)

4. Then you put the almond flour in a plate. (NOTE: Carefully flatten each salmon patty in the palm of your hand and then dip into the almond flour.)
5. Remember, they are fragile so I prefer to place the patty into the flour and then scoop some of the flour on top of the salmon, and then lightly tap it down with my fingers.
6. Meanwhile, you heat a skillet with 2 tablespoons of olive oil.
7. After that, you fry the patties over medium-high heat for a few minutes on each side. Note that they should be cooked through and browned when finished.
8. Finally, you serve two patties with some of our homemade tartar sauce, and veggies.

Conclusion

To lose weight is very easy if you know the process and how to go about it. That is the reason for this Keto cookbook, to help you achieve your weight loss goal in No time. Get in shape while eating the foods you love. Take advantage of this top new healthy and delicious ketogenic recipes provided for you in this book.

Remember, the only bad action you can take is no action at all.

www.ingramcontent.com/pod-product-compliance
Lightning Source LLC
Chambersburg PA
CBHW081724100526
44591CB00016B/2493